A MONSTER
the Size
of the Sun

A MONSTER the Size of the Sun

POEMS
Iryna Klishch

Winner of the 2018
Edna Meudt Memorial Award

National Federation of State Poetry Societies, Inc.
NFSPS Press

A Monster the Size of the Sun © 2018 by Iryna Klishch

All rights reserved. No part of this work may be reproduced or transmitted in any form or by any means, electronic or mechanical, or by use of any information storage or retrieval system, except as may be expressly permitted by the author.

Published April 2018
The National Federation of State Poetry Societies, Inc.
NFSPS Press
www.nfsps.com

Edit and design by Kathy Lohrum Cotton
Cover art, *Summer Abstract* by A. Pobedimskiy
Author's photo by Oksana Kami

Printed in the United States of America
CreateSpace, Charleston, South Carolina

ISBN-13: 978-1986040235
ISBN-10: 1986040232

For my parents

CONTENTS

Foreword ix

Acknowledgments xi

The Kingdom of Heat 1

Mountain of Sun 3

Le Ciel 5

Five Generations of Madness 7

Black Bird, Black Bird 9

Do All Insects Have Organs? 11

Twins 13

Mangata 15

What the Crows Eat 17

Bells, Ringing 19

Author, Iryna Klishch 21

Contest Judge, Benjamin Myers 23

2018 NFSPS CUP Winners 24

NFSPS College Undergraduate Competition 25

NFSPS CUP Chapbook Series 26

National Federation of State Poetry Societies 27

FOREWORD

This poetry collection by Iryna Klishch has been called "a little book by a big talent." It is the work of a young poet, mature beyond her years, who explores writing "viciously, savagely well."

In her own eclectic style, Klishch scatters words and phrases across a page or molds them into couplets, a narrow column, a prose block—all tied together by glimpses of sun. The look of this poetry is as unique as its myriad subjects and its singularly creative author.

The Federation of National Poetry Societies is pleased to introduce Klishch's debut chapbook, *A Monster the Size of the Sun*, our College Undergraduate Poetry (CUP) Competition's 2018 Edna Meudt Memorial Award winner.

Kathy Cotton, Editor
April 2018

ACKNOWLEDGMENTS

Language has taken me by the hand and shown me nothing but light. Thus I am eternally grateful for all those who have not only encouraged my writing, but have allowed me to seize worlds of my own.

Thank you to Denison University and to all the incredible English Department faculty, who have not merely been my professors and mentors, but inspiring, consistent supporters in my love for exploration of voice and poetry. Specifically, David Baker, who has again and again trusted me with my words, even when I did not trust myself, and who has helped me grow into the poet I am today. Thank you to Peter Grandbois, who has introduced me to a world of rich, beautiful literature I could never have found on my own, and who has allowed me to create, destroy, and mold language in ways I could have never dreamed of. And to Anneliese Davis, who has listened to every single one of my stories, and who has taught me the importance of courage and kindness in all that I do.

Thank you to National Federation of State Poetry Societies and to Kathy Cotton for the publication of this chapbook. You have made my wildest dreams come true.

Thank you to my parents. It is without doubt, that without your love I would never have written my first anything. I owe everything to you. Mom, you are the reason I sit heavy with language. Dad, without your strength and knowledge, I would have never found my way to writing in the first place. I promise to finish that novel one day.

Thank you to Yuliya for constantly finding beauty in all that there is. And most importantly to my grandparents—the very first storytellers I encountered, the first to help me fall in love with literature and language and all things true and dear. Each story I tell is a reflection of you. *Дякую за все.*

The Kingdom of Heat

Here, we know the word for *cut*
  but they haven't taught us to slice, to murder: to kill.

Yes, we know rain—paradise, force:
come back to me whispered in the middle of the night

  in the middle of a town that is burning, that is
not on fire: the woman who shaves her head outside the

middle of a town that is burning, that is not on fire: the woman
    who shaves her head outside the public restroom,
  throws it at her son, *here for you, for us*:

war is something we have no language for, and yet
    here: take this cake and bring it to him, for you, from
us. Here, today, it is

    for us, by us, because of us.

Mountain of Sun

Mountain of sun. You thought
        chandelier,
     spilled cider, grease.
You thought olive oil, and
       yellow armchair, an open can of corn—you had
          cut yourself on the rim late, one August.
  Do you remember? Blouse stained,
             washing machine broken,
      your hands in the sink:
the soap, all foam.
  Somebody kept knocking.
       Mountain of sun.
            And you thought electricity:
    your seventh birthday, in that sundress,
       eating pineapple, wearing violet
gloss—your mother's.
         You remember her so differently from
     photographs. Less
    bone, more eye, no hair, just
       skin.
      Mountain of sun,
  and you thought
bathtub. Her: all knees,
      shampooing your roots, golden curls of
          caramel, honey: rinse
     then brush, and dry, and braid.

  Mountain of sun
 and you thought
    apricot, you thought sand:
  lace curtain and chrysanthemum and yolk,
   ocean of fish, field of flowers.
Mountain of sun—why then, have you never thought
  light?

Le Ciel

I have so much to tell you. For one, no, Michelle never got into that one college nor did she ever finish that novella she was always going off about—instead she married the neighbor's son, remember him? He was rather fat and always carried around that harmonica, yeah, the one that we kept making fun of him about, so anyways she got married to him somewhere in June and they had this wedding out in the middle of that field, you know the one—the one where we first kissed, well anyways she married him, I think, out of spite, you see, her papa was always going off about how she would never amount to nothing and I guess one day she just had enough, and it's not like her fella was anything special, but he did get to inherit his granddaddy's hardware store so they're living off somewhere in the middle of Vermont now, and I tried writing to her just the other week, but apparently there's no address. Gone. It's like she disappeared into thin air. Isn't that strange? She was always going off about doing something great, something miraculous, something that happens when you chop off your tongue. Remember that? She used that expression back before the war started? God, that was long ago. What else? I've decided that there is no way Juliette is going to stop seeing that boy she's been seeing. He drinks a lot and last week I found that pretty sun dress, the one with the yellow hem stitched by the knees? Yeah, thrown in the wash with a giant wine stain on it and I guess it shouldn't really take me by surprise anymore, except that it reminded me of the time that we went to see the windmills, you remember that? You took me in the middle of the night, I was so scared that Mama would wake up and make me spend the day with her at church again, but I wanted to see you and we did it. I guess, before the war, everything was a lot less and a lot more. Once, when you weren't looking, I stuffed those raspberries in your coat pockets. I loved how angry you got. I love how much we laughed after. There is something so special about how time passes. Everything is different and yet the air tastes the same. I write, like some people play piano, viciously and sometimes so slow you can hear the notes scatter across the air until someone's skin touches it. I think if you ever came back, I would have told you that there are some people who think about the sky, and some people who want to touch it.

Five Generations of Madness

Maria places bowls of water all over the house
          so the flies can drown in peace. She is fat,
tongue heavy with lemon, honey-dew,
          French bread—hair dried of vinaigrette, egg
yolk. She keeps forgetting to wash her hands. Her mama, Tess,
          the only brown beautician on the West Side,
              had her tongue sliced by the village's priest,
she had forgotten to pray before supper   she left him
             no choice. Maria
        honey-eyed
     wears aprons
and nude stockings, gold hoop earrings, red lipstick. Her
          daughter Janice rings her a quarter past
noon, no answer and she
          leaves a message, "Mama,
Mama call me, something's
        happened."

There are snakes in the bathtub,
only now, now nobody looks for
      them. Only now, Maria is busy, there
are too many   weeds in the garden—how will
     the bees   know where to look?

Janice is thin, eyes like saw-dust,
    skin of milk, tooth-
        aches are common, she has a

    daughter, Jane? Maybe Elizabeth,
  are those Victorian names?
                And when the telephone stops,
          Janice presses her palm to her
              mouth, licks it wet and bites

hard. Tess is in the sea—drowned at two, nobody saw
  her after church that Sunday, nobody asked why she
      was wearing black lace.
Maria puts salt on the napkin. There is classical music, she
      is wearing Chanel perfume, a white bra, skin made
of wax. She takes the first of them,
              gently, places her
on the napkin. Makes sure of the wings.
              Then only, can there be flight.

Black Bird, Black Bird

There are magenta swans
floating in the sea tonight.
I can hear them, their brass
bellies against the pink glow
of the salt water, the sun a
splinter in the depth of the
starving sky. I watch as they
sway, and am reminded of
the time I swallowed the juice
from the jar of pickles, too
much, how Ma made me clean
the toilet bowl, how much I
hated the smell, the taste of
the sick. And after, the night,
so blue, I could hear the cry
of the bird. In the morning
the gape of the hawk, his
feathers spilled across the
field, a filter of an unwept
tame, only oil left within the
rose bushes. I often thought,
how beautiful it would be
to hold the heart of the white
bird, to put the life of it
between my teeth, press it
against the gum: chew, bite,

then swallow. Perhaps the next morning I would find beak, no mouth, all wing. But, there is a cancer in the silence of sin. And so, I would awaken to find the blackness of the fur, covered against hip and thigh, hidden between calf and lip, already in flight, the black swan.

Do All Insects Have Organs?

The entire town goes to mass early, dead dandelions
    in a vase. Our ankles scratch carpet, are teeth
        muted in copper.
    Who's going to pick up that telephone? It rings,
then the crash. Turn off the television, we don't want to
        hear about the murders anymore.
    She was seventeen. All summer, there had been
the rumors she was seeing an older man. Her mama, a
taxi driver,   when they told her,
        silence.
When the rain ate those purple flowers, the kettle
    was boiled for two.
      Miss, miss—we have to ask
      you some questions. Did you see anything?
    Who was she with?
What was she like? Which picture do you want to show?
Her mama, all smiles. Jessica,
      what a dear.
    She spilled Coca-Cola all over Simone's yellow
sundress. When I asked, hmm,
    when I asked if it was an accident: No, Mama, no.
      She had just gotten
        her ears pierced, two diamond studs—
    lost them a week later. She
loved
      ginger ale, her plants. There was some sort

of infection one summer. She kept
        her hair long, her feet   always
          cold.

     Cold. Where is she now? No, I
can't identify her body.
Have someone
          else do it. Have
the priest.

   The entire town goes to mass early, drinks the wine, forgets about
the prayer.   Then: Where is the copy of the Bible? Can someone find it?
     What does it say about insects? Do they eat human flesh, which
       part are they after? The heart or the lung—
          Do all insects have organs?

Twins

The chemical spill left the tomatoes burnt, their necks
wet and dry in the winter ground, their stomachs rough

in the heat of the sun. Today, the birds sleep. I am a child
who thinks of death often. It is he, who visits me between

the small lapses of shifting seasons, it is he I see when Ma
is chewing nuts, when Michael shows us the pond behind

the campground, tells us to take off our top, and there is
so much lime in the air I ask what happened to the smoke.

This is not political. In October, the leaves forget that
they must undress, strip themselves bare, a favor that the

earth asks, one that even the worms have grown to keenly
understand. The collision happens so suddenly we mistake

it for air. There was no sign of the storm. Two breaths of
lightning, an orchestra dedicated only to cough, to the sharp

inhale of fur, wheat, grass. I think I can see them, the small
patches of white swans dancing, but even they have been

carved of their feather, even they have been skinned of their
wing. It is the lightning that finally collapses the branch, stirs

its fall through cracks of dirt, filed underneath crust and rib,
molded with red cicadas and blue ants, the Queen of the Night

in bloom.

Mangata

Magnolia ate dragon fruit and fish, cooked marigolds
      in a white pot, waited for the steam to hover over
  her skin, like vapor, smoke. She had just written
her first novella, a princess had become taken with a
      peasant, Gustave: the King's
florist. He had given her narcissus, poppies,
carnations. He had given her coral and cyan, magentas and
      pastels. They decorated powder rooms, floated in the
  tub; lilacs and violets filled the room with hints of
nectar and jasmine, sweet
      spices of air licking at teeth. When war
  began,
  even
the Queen began to pray. It was always humid, as
      if light itself was turning sour. Magnolia's favorite
  scene was the garden at dawn,
the princess wearing nothing but rubies, her naked
      body pressed against
  cobblestone, the sun—electric emerald.
                      It was the
morning after she received news of her
    lover passing in
      battle; the maids had left out bread
and raisins for her, a glass filled with soup made of carp,
      some almonds. But the princess lay there
until the guards
      came, moved her limp body from the ground
    up
    up.

Inside,
silk sheets grazed her ankles, wrapping
tightly around her neck, the breasts. She could
smell it, the color

daffodil.

How wonderful, she thought, *it is to love another
body, another mouth*. It was that same night,
the princess wrote a poem:
a women named Magnolia sat hunched
overlooking a terrace, writing. She titled the art,
Mangata.

What the Crows Eat

The birds are eating pieces of the sky, but nobody knows this yet. At church, the priest is chewing the word *sin* like hot candle wax and I can feel it warm against my teeth so I avoid all eye contact. When I was only a child, someone handed me a violin and told me to play. I guess they did the same with my lungs. Who was the first person to eat their own hands? Who was the first to touch another's heart? My skirt is itching my thighs, but I wear the air like a fur coat. Someone is sneezing, yet no one says bless you. What did Michelangelo dream of? After, we go to a Bistro and eat hot soup and oysters. I can't stop staring at his hands. On the bus ride home, a young child asks for quarters and everyone pretends they can't hear. Her eyes are the color of sky before wet thunder licks it.

At home, I fill the bathtub with brown water. At night, I dream of black crows eating dandelions, a yellow yolk so bright, it burns me.

Bells, Ringing

We walk through the apricot trees, the wool
    skirt rough against my knees, I have not

stopped sneezing since the blossom of spring, you ask
    if I remember the fur, the black spider inside

the swollen narcissus, him aching to be felt by the sun,
    to be stripped of the skin, *a monster*, between

our teeth. Today, I wait for rain. When it does not come,
    I call my mother, who has already set the table,

who has already called the neighbor's son, asked him about
    the leaking faucet, why the dog won't stop barking,

the fence that Pa always said he'd paint, never did; when I
    met Jack he was only a boy. Today, the rain does not

come. We walk through the apricot trees, I am all teeth, hair
    uncombed, you ask if I am alright, I tell you the

story of my grandmother, a woman whose mouth I wear
    like jewelry, whose tongue I grow, never bite.

She was only fourteen when the soldiers came, and at
    first, she only remembers the rotten potatoes.

How her ma made them gather the fields, bring them
    back, empty buckets, cook them raw, feed the children.

Watch as they got sick, not enough water for them all.
    Then again, that very same week. The children must

eat. We walk through the apricot trees, and when I tell you
    goodbye, you look into the sun, a burning so fierce,

I think you've already gone.

AUTHOR, IRYNA KLISHCH

Iryna Klishch was born in Nadvirna, Ukraine, but grew up in Illinois, outside Chicago. As a Denison University senior, completing a BA in English (Creative Writing), Klishch received the NFSPS Edna Meudt Award for undergraduate poetry. She was also winner of the Stony Brook Short Fiction Prize, and her work has appeared in various literary magazines. Through her writing, Klishch says, she wishes to inspire, to create, to destroy, to challenge, to light. She hopes her words find you.

CONTEST JUDGE, BENJAMIN MYERS

Benjamin Myers was the 2015-2016 Oklahoma State Poet Laureate. His most recent book is *Lapse Americana* (New York Quarterly Books, 2013), and he won the Oklahoma Book Award for Poetry for his first book, *Elegy for Trains* (Village Books Press, 2010). *Black Sunday: The Dust Bowl Sonnets* is forthcoming from Lamar University Press. His poems have appeared in *The Yale Review, Ninth Letter, 32 Poems, Image, Tupelo Quarterly,* and many other journals. Myers has also written about poetry and poetics for publications including *World Literature Today, Books and Culture, Oklahoma Today,* and *First Things*, as well as for academic journals.

He is a frequent and sought-after reader at many festivals and conferences and was recently awarded a Tennessee Williams Scholarship from the Sewanee Writers' Conference. With a Ph.D. from Washington University in St. Louis, Myers teaches creative writing and literature at Oklahoma Baptist University, where he is the Crouch-Mathis Professor of Literature.

2018 NFSPS CUP WINNERS

Edna Meudt Memorial Award
Iryna Klishch
Denison University, Granville, OH
A Monster the Size of the Sun

Florence Kahn Memorial Award
Catherine Valdez
Columbia University, New York City, NY
Imperial Debris in Quisqueya and Beyond

1st Honorable Mention
Kara Applegate
Gordon College, Wenham, MA
for "On Certain Mornings"

2nd Honorable Mention
Juliana Chang
Stanford University, Palo Alto, CA
for "Inheritance"

3rd Honorable Mention
Hannah Isaac
University of Arizona, Tucson, AZ
for "Puppet Show"

4th Honorable Mention
Heather Bellinger
Corban University, Salem, OR
for "Cut Gravity's Cord"

5th Honorable Mention
Christie Clause
Gordon College, Wenham, MA
for "Things to Remember"

NFSPS COLLEGE UNDERGRADUATE POETRY COMPETITION

In 1988 NFSPS planned the addition of a college-level scholarship, subsequently named in memory of NFSPS charter member and past president Edna Meudt. In 1999, with a generous bequest by Florence Kahn, the NFSPS Scholarship Award expanded to include a second competition, the Florence Kahn Memorial Award.

Now named the College Undergraduate Poetry (CUP) Competition, the annual contest is open to students working toward a degree in an accredited U.S. college or university. Winners of the Meudt and Kahn awards each receive $500, publication and 75 free copies of their chapbook, a $300 travel stipend to attend and read at the NFSPS convention, and other perks.

Contest guidelines and submission dates are posted on the NFSPS website, www.nfsps.com.

> NFSPS CUP Committee:
>
> Chair, Shirley Blackwell, New Mexico
> Editor, Kathy Cotton, Illinois

NFSPS CUP CHAPBOOK SERIES

The CUP series of winning chapbooks
also includes:

Imperial Debris in Quisqueya and Beyond
Catherine Valdez

A Natural Cacophony
Sydney Lo

Exhales
Brian Selkirk

Elegy for Your Eyes
Anna Goodson

But Sometimes I Remember
Michael Welch

The Hole of Everything Nebraska
Max Siefert

Here I Go, Torching
Carlina Duan

Earlier CUP series books are available at
www.nfsps.com

NATIONAL FEDERATION OF STATE POETRY SOCIETIES

The National Federation of State Poetry Societies (NFSPS) is a nonprofit organization, exclusively educational and literary. NFSPS offers linguistic and professional contexts that appeal to the mind and spirit and is dedicated to the furtherance of poetry on the national level and to uniting poets in the bonds of fellowship and understanding.

Membership in NFSPS is provided to members of any affiliated state poetry society (see www.nfsps.com). Poets in states without an affiliated society may join state societies as at-large members.

Poetry competitions sponsored by NFSPS include:
- 50 annual poetry contests with cash prizes totaling more than $6,000, including a grand prize of $1,000.
- Stevens Poetry Manuscript Competition for a full-length poetry collection.
- College Undergraduate Poetry Competition with the Florence Kahn Memorial and the Edna Meudt Memorial awards going to the top two chapbook manuscript winners.
- Manningham Trust Student Poetry Contest for winners advancing from state-level competitions.
- The BlackBerryPeach Prizes for Poetry: Spoken and Heard, for print and spoken-word poetry.

For more information on contests or membership, visit the website, www.nfsps.com.

Made in the USA
Lexington, KY
09 April 2018